Geography Starts

CORAL REEFS

Claire Llewellyn

Heinemann Library
Chicago, Illinois

© 2000 Reed Educational & Professional Publishing
Published by Heinemann Interactive Library,
an imprint of Reed Educational & Professional Publishing,
Chicago, IL

Customer Service 888-454-2279

Visit our website at www.heinemannlibrary.com

Designed by David Oakley

Illustrations by Hardlines and Jo Brooker
Printed and bound in China

07 06
10 9 8 7 6 5

Library of Congress Cataloging-in-Publication Data
Llewellyn, Claire.
    Coral reefs / Claire Llewellyn.
        p. cm. – (Geography starts)
    Includes bibliographical references (p.) and index.
    Summary: Explores the phenomenon of coral reefs, discussing their formation,
location, and types, as well as threats to coral reefs and efforts to preserve them.
    ISBN 1-57572-203-8 (lib. bdg.)   ISBN 1-58810-969-0 (pbk. bdg.)
    1. Coral reefs and islands—Juvenile literature. [1. Corals. 2. Coral reefs and islands.] I.
Title. II. Series.
GB461.L554 2000
551.42'4—dc21
                                                            99-053328

Acknowledgments
The Publishers would like to thank the following for permission to reproduce photographs:
Bruce Coleman/Timothy O'Keefe, p. 20; Bruce Coleman/Larry Lipsky, p. 29; FLPA/G. Lebois p.5, Bruce Coleman/Ian
Cartwright, p. 7; Bruce Coleman/Silvestris, p. 8; Bruce Coleman/David B. Fleetham p.10; NASA/Johnson Space Center,
pp. 22, 24,26; Oxford Scientific Films/David B. Fleetham, pp .6, 16, Oxford Scientific Films/Mark Webster, p. 14; Oxford
Scientific Films/Laurence Gould, p. 18; Robert Harding Picture Library, p.21; Still Pictures/Fred Bavendam, p. 4; Still
Pictures/Gerard & Margi Moss, pp. 9, 11, 13; Still Pictures/Truchet-Unep, p. 12; Still Pictures/Yves Lefevre, p. 15; Still
Pictures/Norbert Wu, p. 17; Still Pictures/Alberto Garcias/Christian Aid, p. 19; Still Pictures/Roland Seitre, p. 28.

Cover photograph reproduced with permission of Still Pictures.

Some words are shown in bold, **like this**. You can find
out what they mean by looking in the glossary.

Contents

What Is a Coral Reef?

A coral reef looks like a huge rock garden under the sea. A reef is made by billions of tiny sea animals called **corals**.

These corals look like brightly colored plants growing in the water.

A coral reef looks like rocks under the water.

A coral reef is made of **limestone** left in the ocean by the corals.

How Do Reefs Grow?

Corals have soft bodies. They grow hard **skeletons** to protect themselves. Each tiny skeleton is shaped like a cup.

Corals grow in many different shapes and colors. This is antler coral.

This coral reef has been growing for thousands of years.

When old corals die, their **limestone** skeletons stay on the reef. New corals grow on top of them. A reef begins to grow.

Where Do Reefs Grow?

These coral reefs are around islands in the Indian Ocean.

Most coral reefs grow in warm, shallow water around islands or along the **coast**.

The coral reefs help to **protect** the coast from high waves and stormy seas.

Waves break on the reef, but the water between the reef and the land is calm.

Barrier Reefs

Some coral reefs follow the coastline but lie in deeper water farther from shore. They are called **barrier** reefs because they **protect** the land from the sea.

The Great Barrier Reef off Australia is as high as a 40-story building.

The waters in a lagoon are calmer than the choppy sea.

The sea water between the reef and the shore is called a **lagoon.** It is protected from the wind and ocean waves.

A Coral Island

Many islands are the **peaks** of **volcanoes** under the sea. Sometimes a volcano sinks down below the waves because of movements deep inside the earth.

This island is the top of a volcano.
A coral reef is growing all around it.

There was once an island in the middle of this ring of coral. But now it has sunk below the waves and disappeared.

A ring of coral like this is called an atoll.

Rain Forests of the Sea

Coral reefs are sometimes called the rain forests of the sea. This is because they are home to thousands of different living things.

This coral reef is crowded and full of life.

These gray sharks hunt the animals that live on this coral reef.

Small animals live on the reef, feeding on smaller animals or plants. Larger animals visit the reef to find food.

Reefs in Danger

Rough seas can batter
and break a coral reef.

Coral is hard and stony, but it is still easy
to break. It cracks during storms when it
is pounded by the sea.

The crown-of-thorns starfish feeds on coral. In one day, a crown-of-thorns starfish can eat enough coral to cover a small table. This much coral can take one hundred years to grow.

The crown-of-thorns starfish can cause a lot of damage to a reef.

Human Damage

Some divers make money by collecting and selling pieces of coral.

People also damage coral reefs. **Corals** die when people stand on a reef, knock it with an **anchor,** or break off pieces to sell.

Divers catch the animals and fish that live in coral reefs and sell them. Some of the fish are now very rare because they have been hunted too much.

This diver has caught a tropical fish to sell as a pet.

Saving the Reefs

Coral reefs need to be **protected.** One way of doing this is to turn them into underwater **marine parks**. Then they are protected by law.

This coral reef is in the U.S. Virgin Islands. It is now a marine park.

These people are learning to dive so that they can visit a coral reef.

People visit the reefs and see the animals and plants that live there. They learn how to protect the reefs.

Reef Map 1

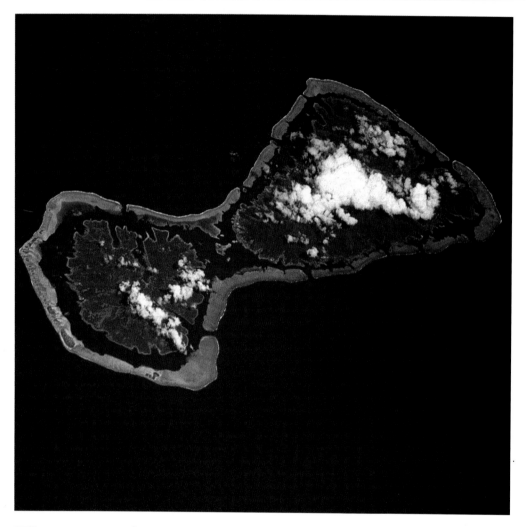

This is a photo of a small island. It was taken from a **satellite**. Coral reefs have grown all around the island. There are **lagoons** between the reefs and the shore.

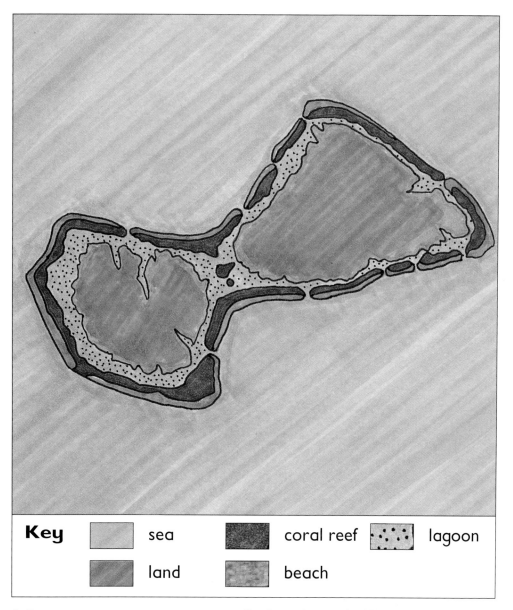

Key

⬜	sea	⬛	coral reef	⬜ lagoon	
⬜	land	⬜	beach		

Maps are pictures of the land. This map shows us the same place as the photo. The coral reefs are shown in purple. You can see beaches around the reefs. They are orange.

Reef Map 2

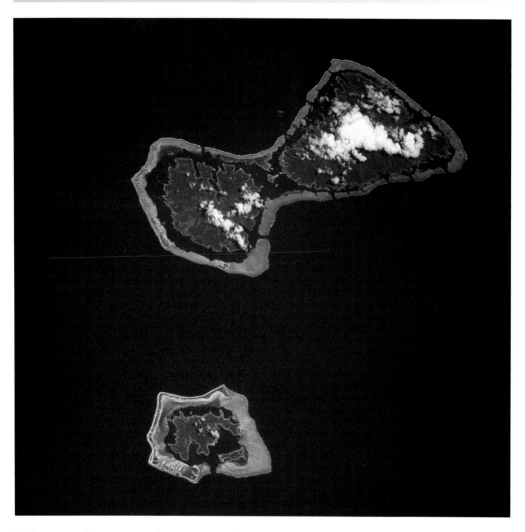

This photo shows the same island. The island looks smaller, but you can see more of the sea around it. You can see a second island. It has coral around it, too.

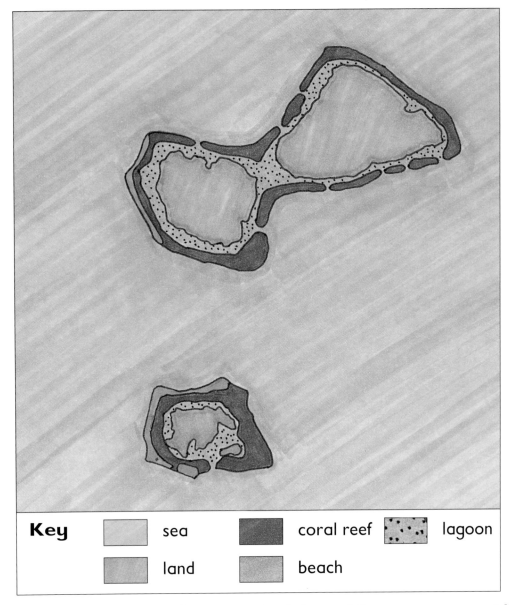

| Key | | sea | | coral reef | | lagoon |
| | | land | | beach | | |

On the map, the sea is blue. You can see the spotted blue between the coral reef and the land. This is called a **lagoon**. The water here is shallow and sheltered.

Reef Map 3

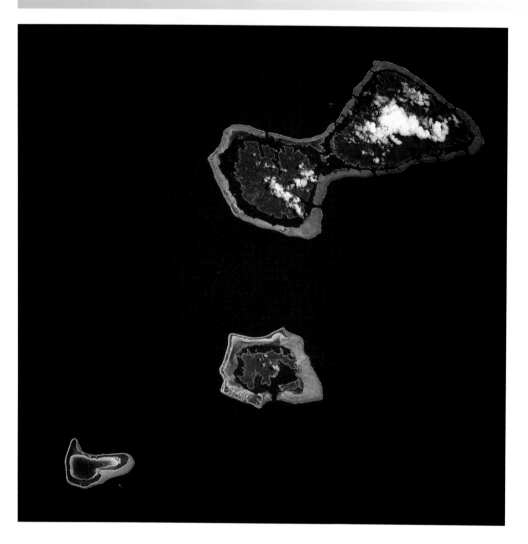

In this photo, the islands look even smaller. Now you can see a third coral island nearby. This third island is made only of a ring of coral reef. The islands look like big dots in the sea.

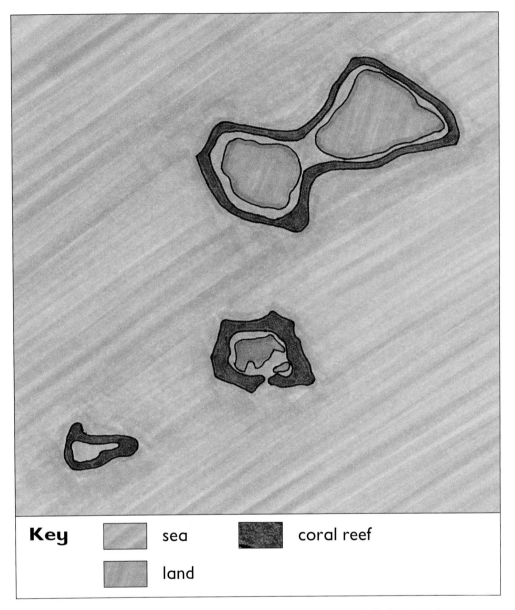

Key

☐ sea	◼ coral reef
☐ land	

Maps give useful information. With this map, it is easy to see how far the islands are from one another. You can also see which island is the biggest.

Amazing Reef Facts

The Great Barrier Reef is a long line of reefs off the **coast** of **Australia.** Altogether, it is half as large as the state of Texas. It can be seen from the moon!

The wrinkly coral on the left of the picture is called brain coral.

This coral reef is growing near Florida. Florida is cooler than most places **corals** grow, but the ocean around it is warm. It flows up from the hotter parts of the world.

Glossary

anchor   heavy piece of metal connected to a chain that boats drop into the water to stay in one place

barrier thing that blocks other things out

coast   land that is at the edge of the ocean

coral   tiny animal that lives in the sea and that leaves behind part of its body when it dies

lagoon   sheltered shallow water that lies between a coral reef and the shore

limestone   kind of rock that is easily cut and shaped

marine park   underwater place protected by law to keep it safe and beautiful

peak   very top of a mountain

protect   to keep safe

satellite special machine that goes around the earth in space taking photographs of the earth

skeleton   hard part of an animal's body that protects it and gives it its shape

volcano   hill or mountain made by hot rocks that come out of an opening in the earth

More Books to Read

Earle, Sylvia. *Hello, Fish!: Visiting the Coral Reef.* Washington, D.C.: National Geographic Society, 1999.

Leonard, Tom. *Here Is the Coral Reef.* New York: Hyperion, 1998.

An older reader can help you with these books:

Owens, Caleb. *Coral Reefs.* Chanhassen, Minn.: The Child's World, Inc., 1998

Telford, Carole, and Rod Theodorou. *Inside a Coral Reef.* Des Plaines, Ill.: Heinemann Library, 1998.

Index